I0392650

VOLUME 1

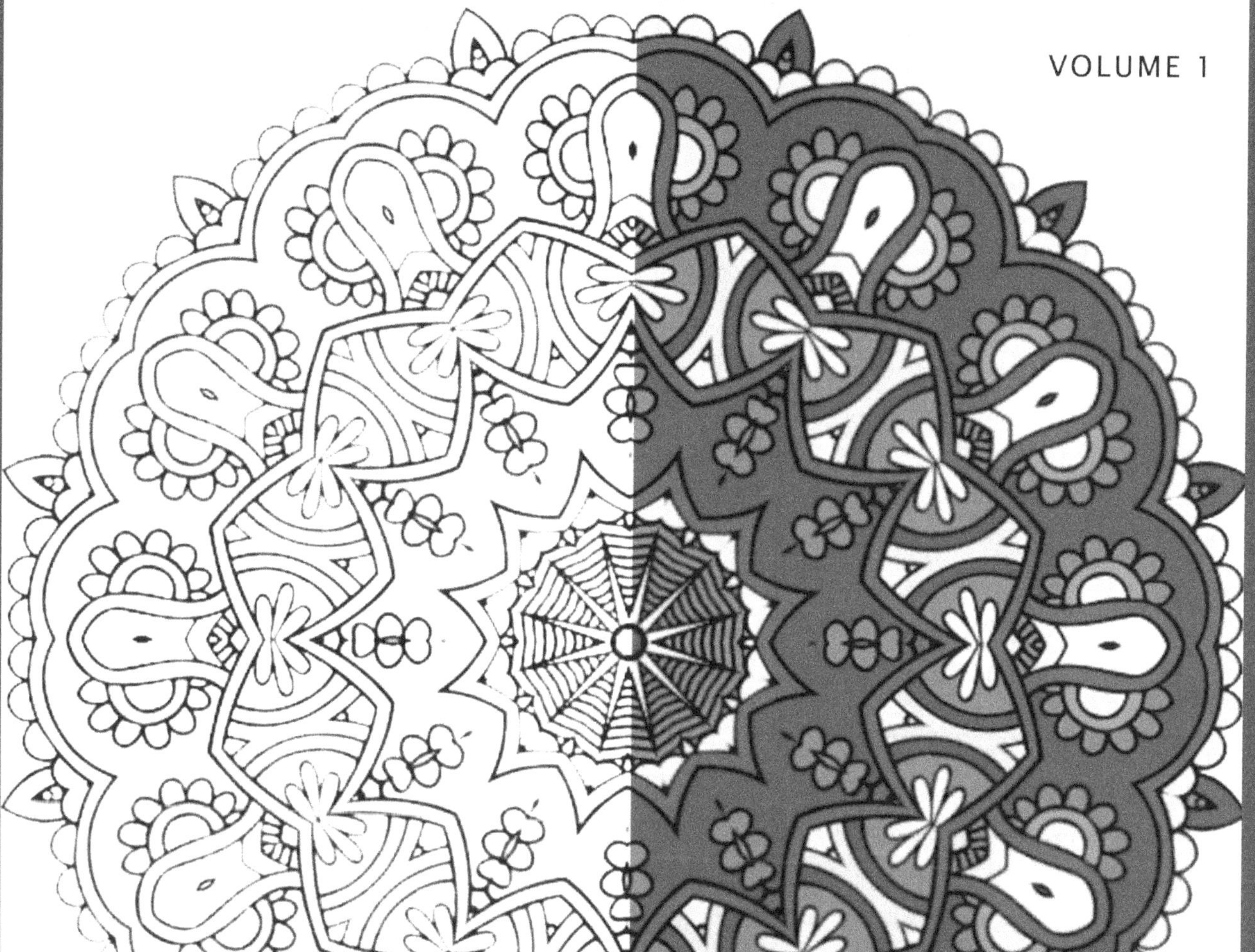

FLOWER MANDALAS

COLORING BOOK FOR ADULTS

COLOR TEST PAGE

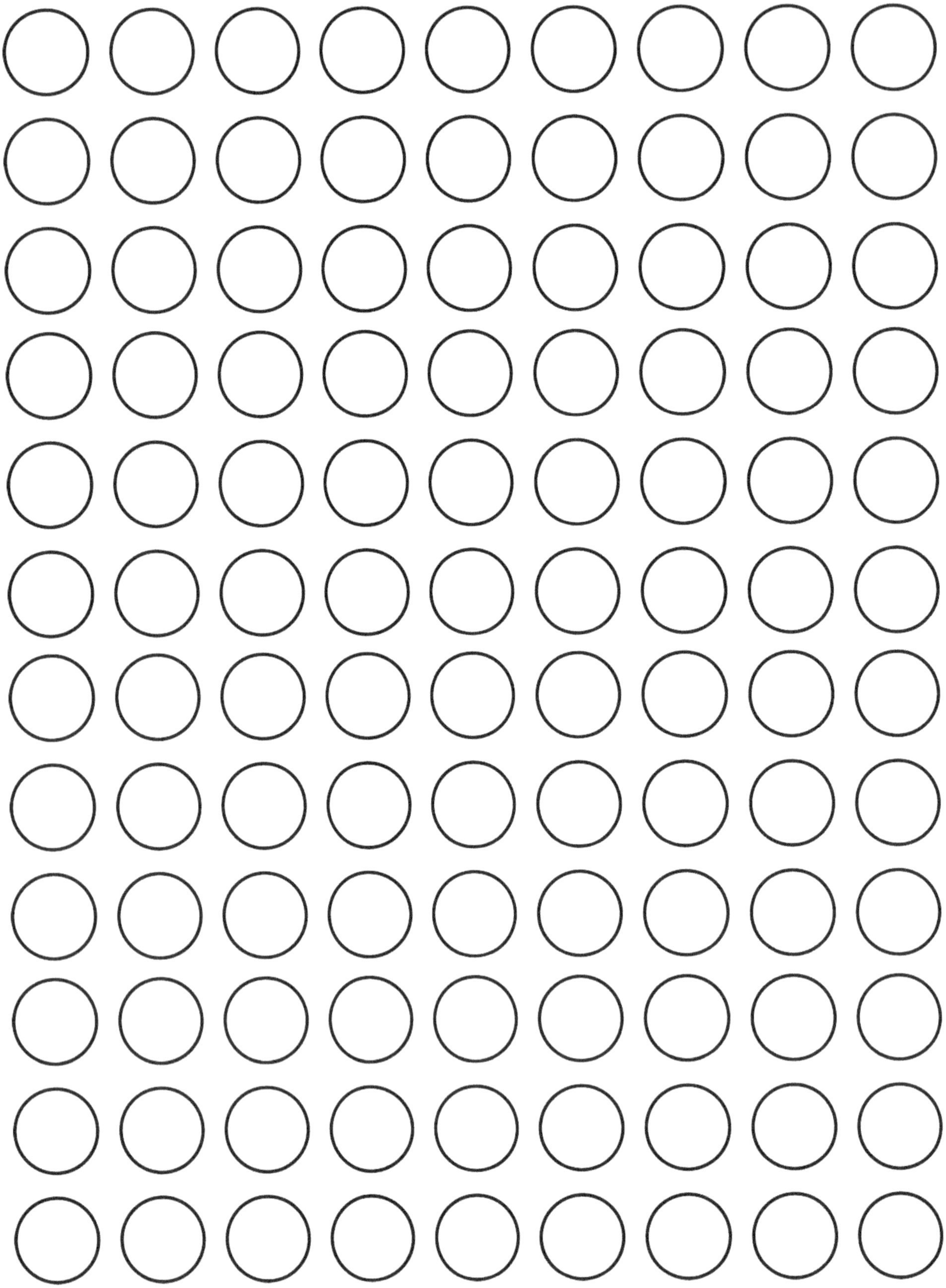

COLOR TEST PAGE

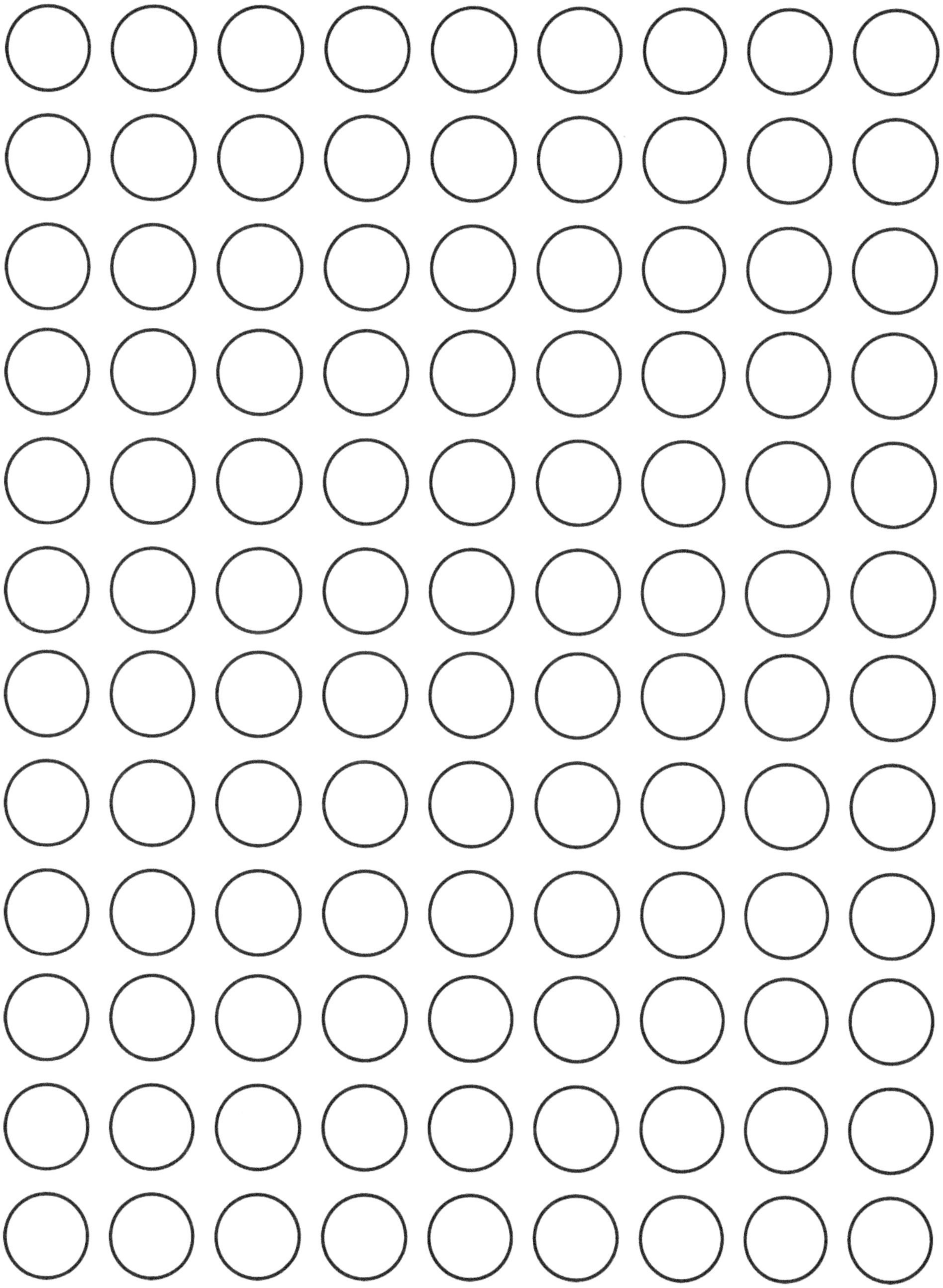

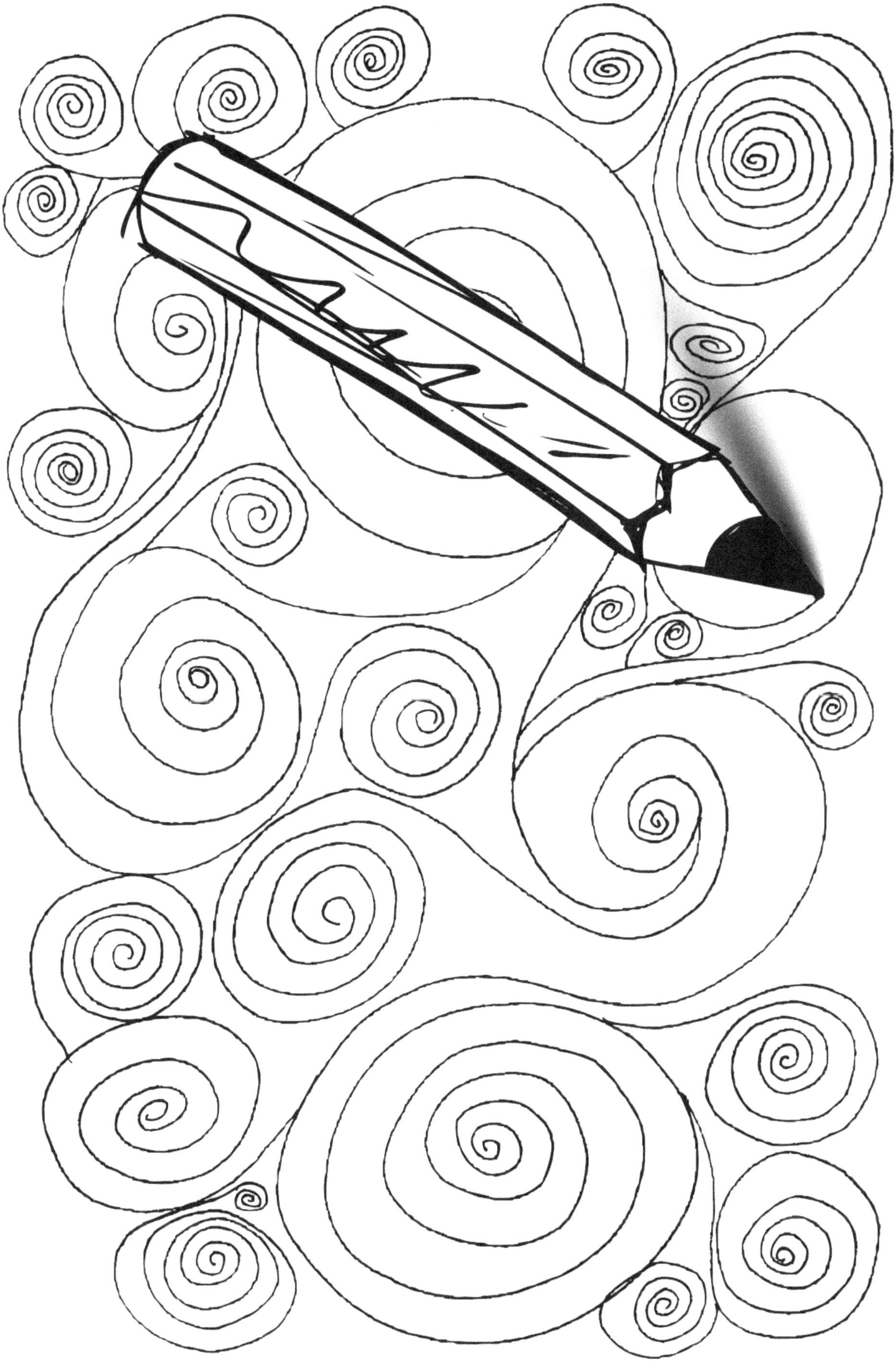

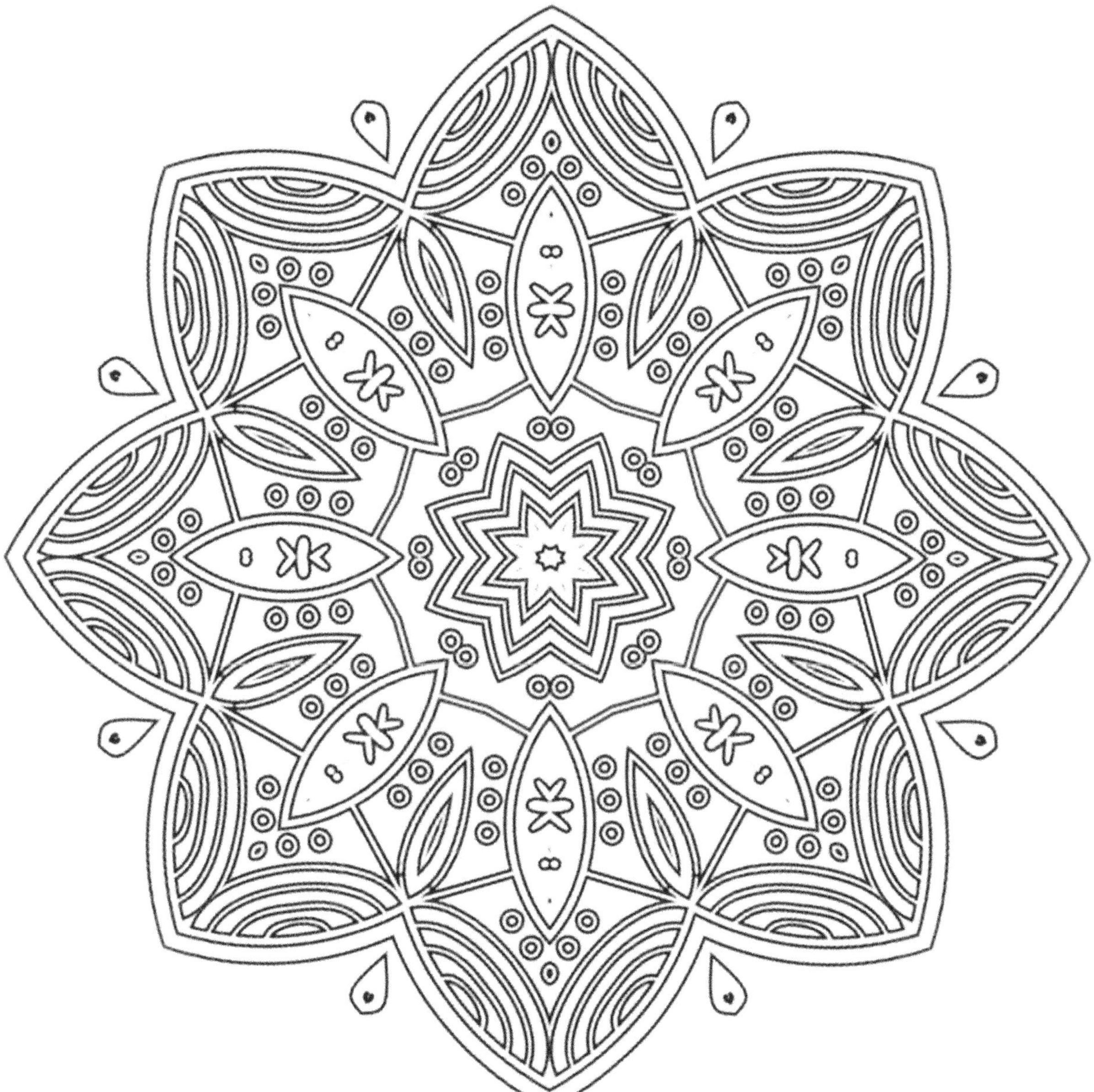

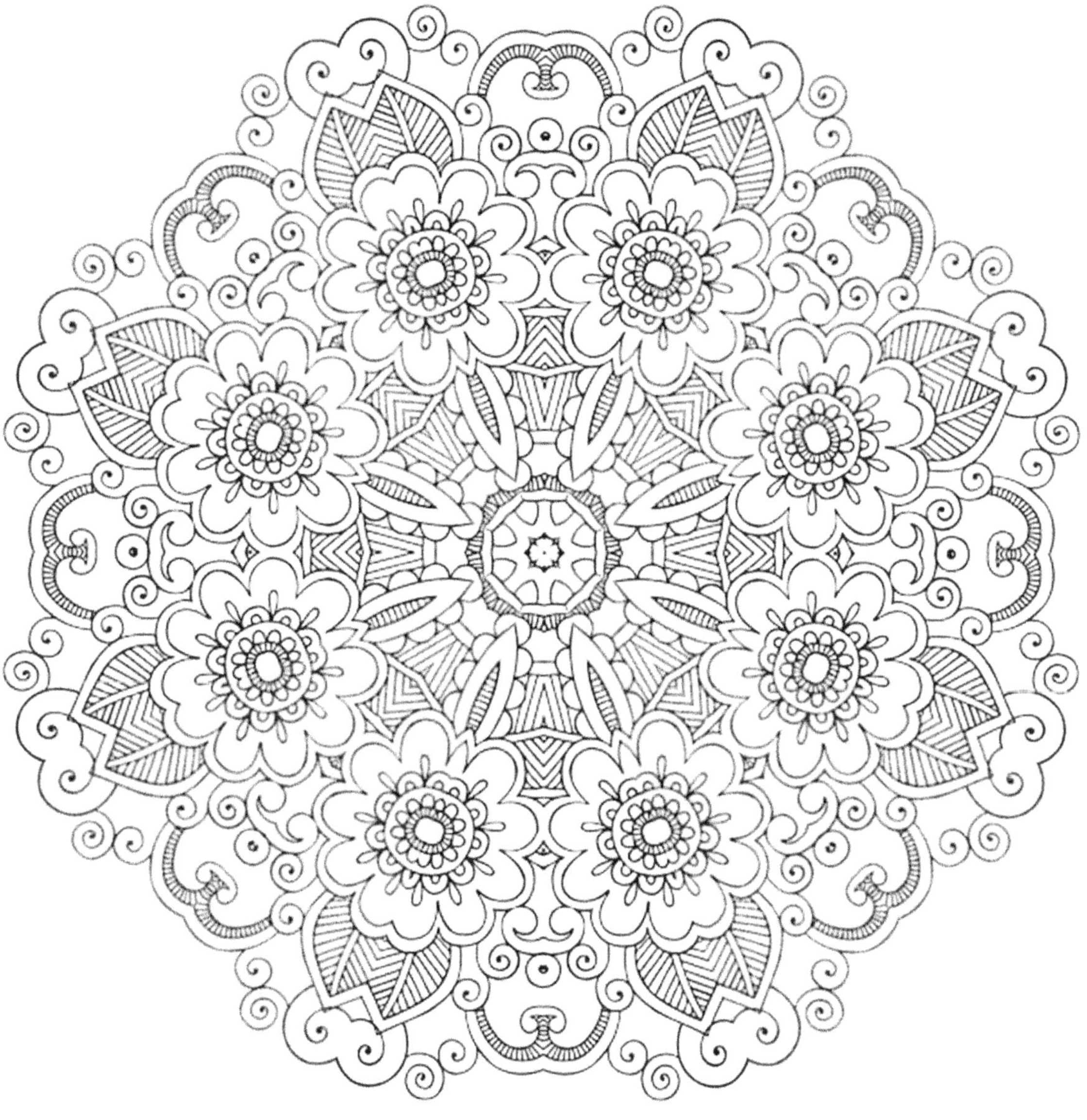

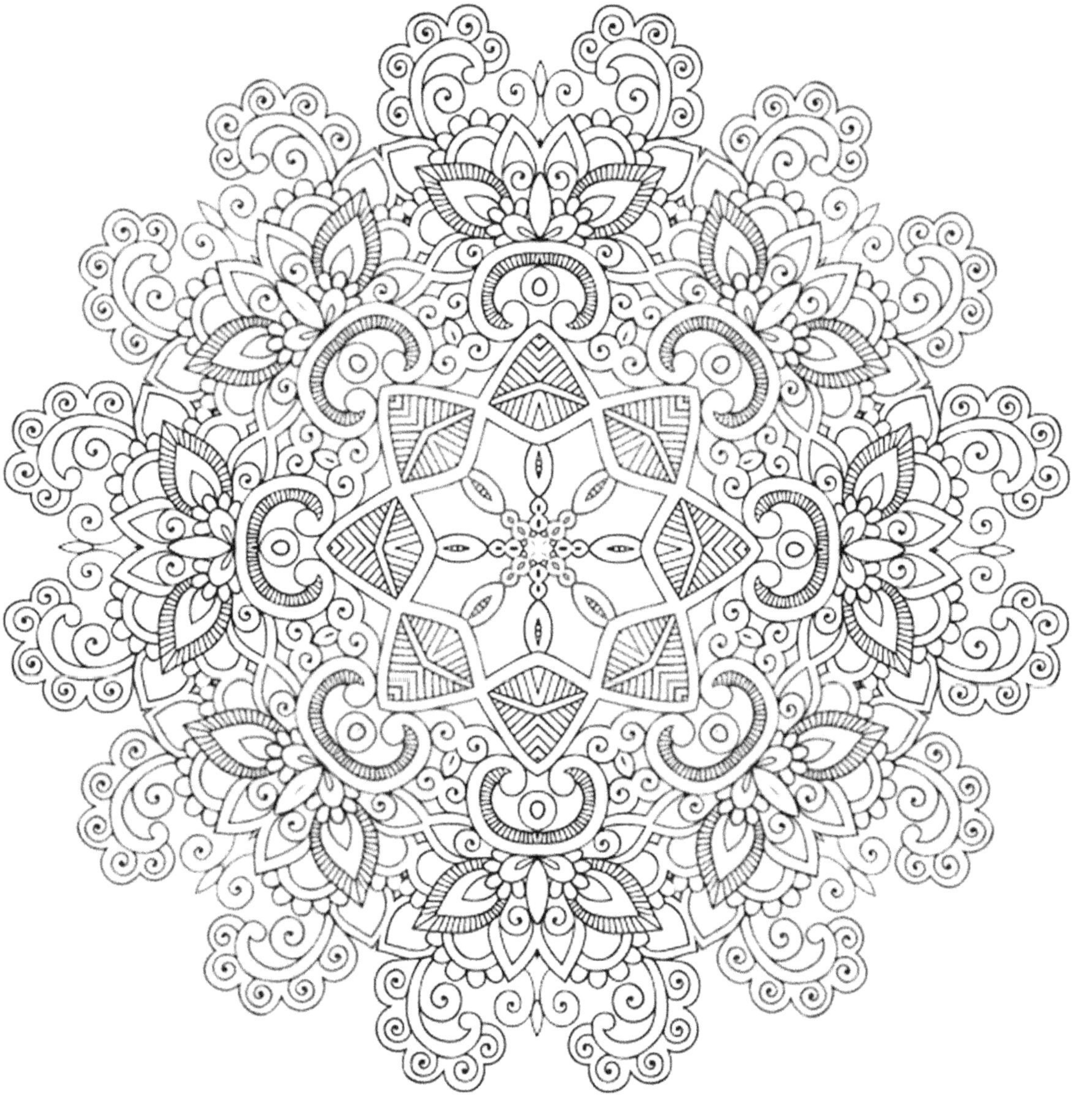

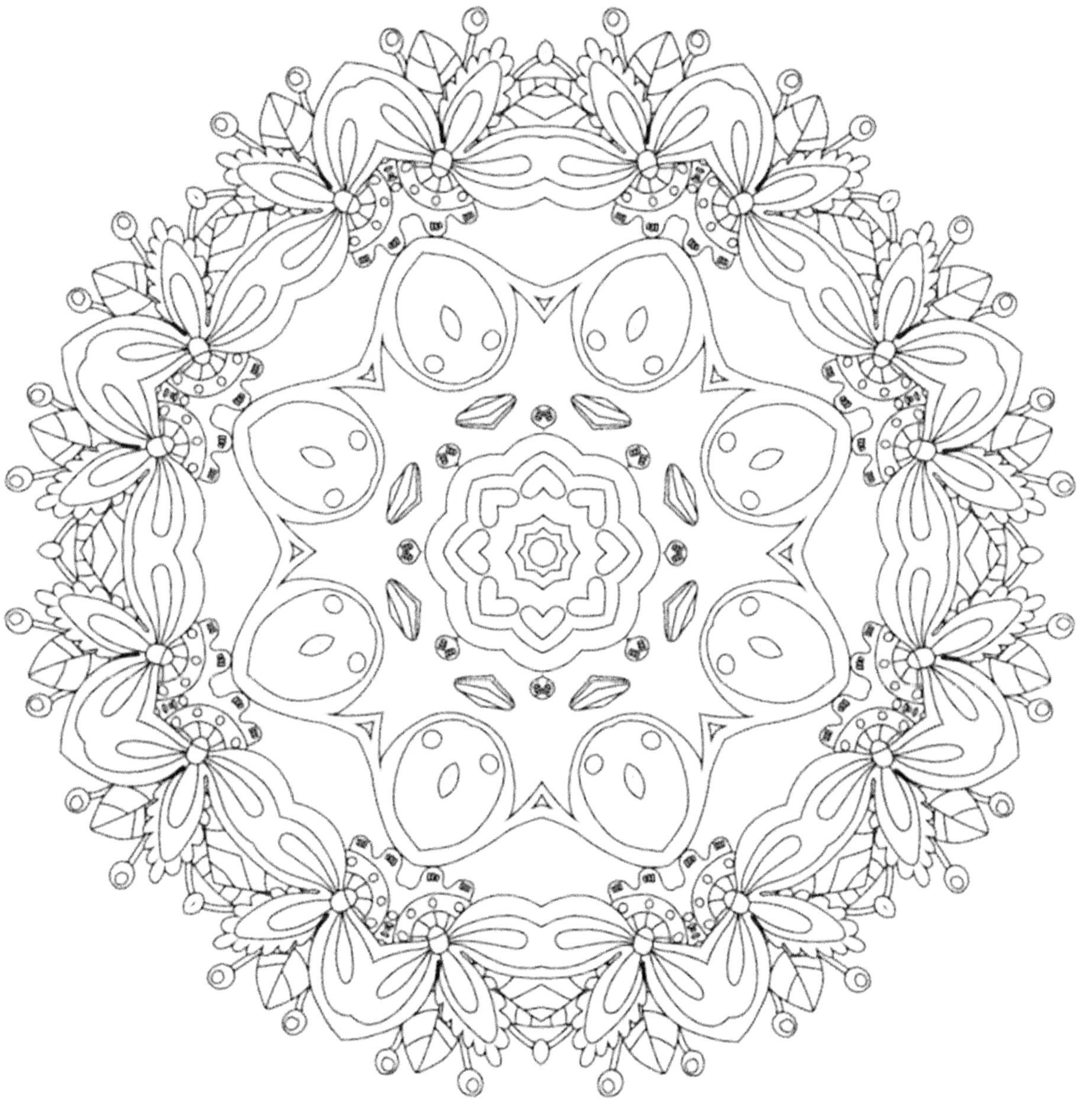

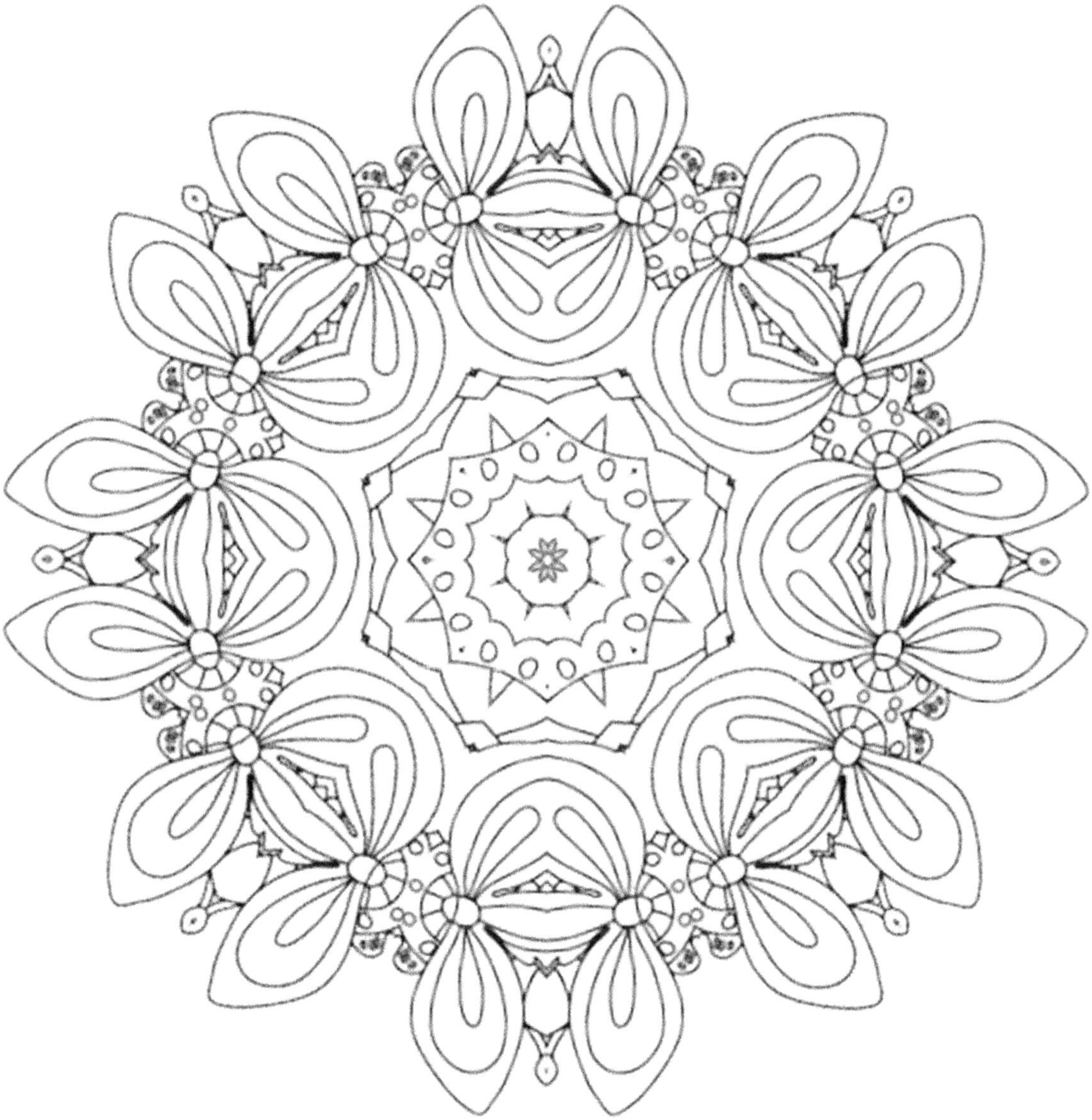

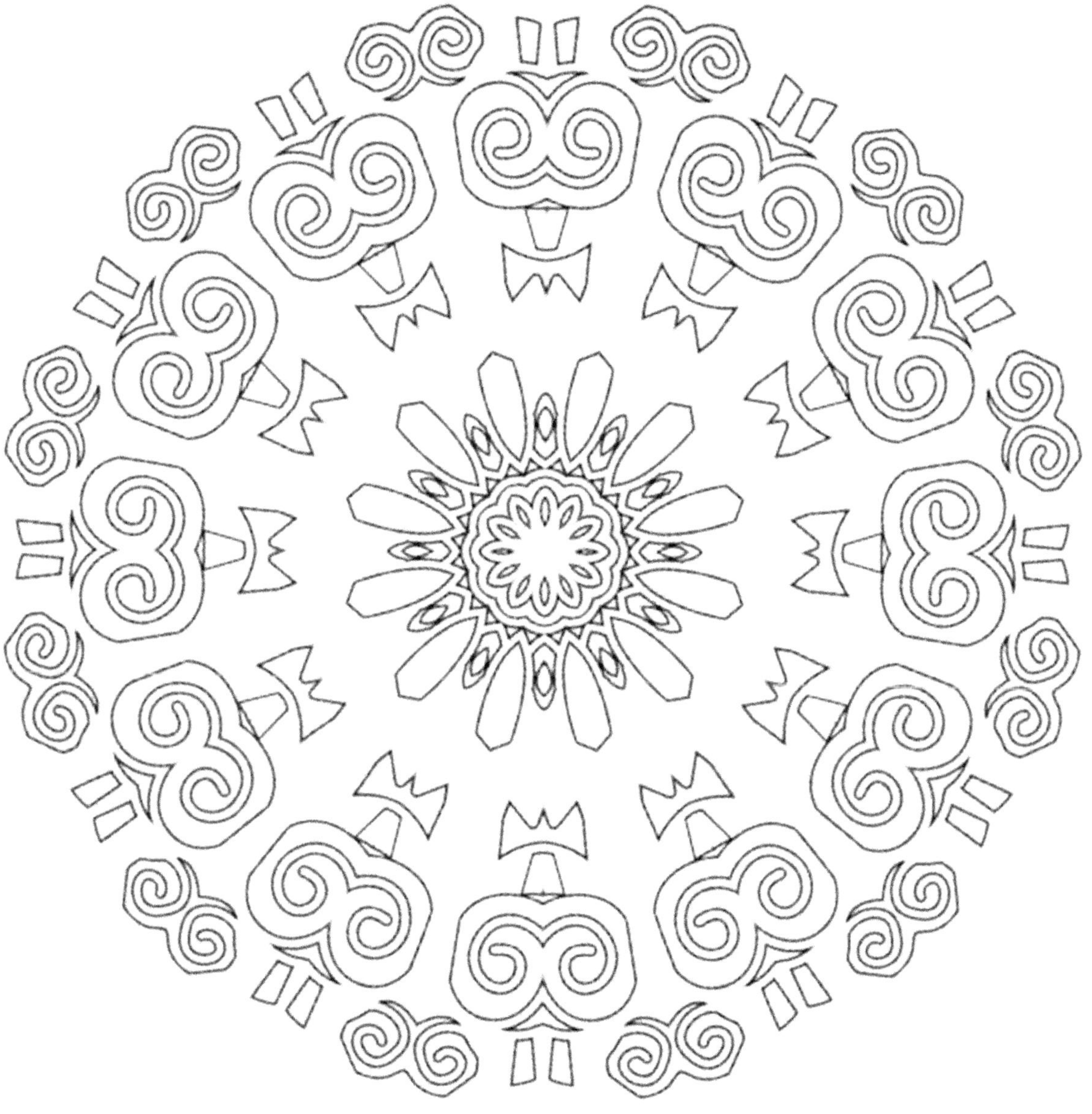

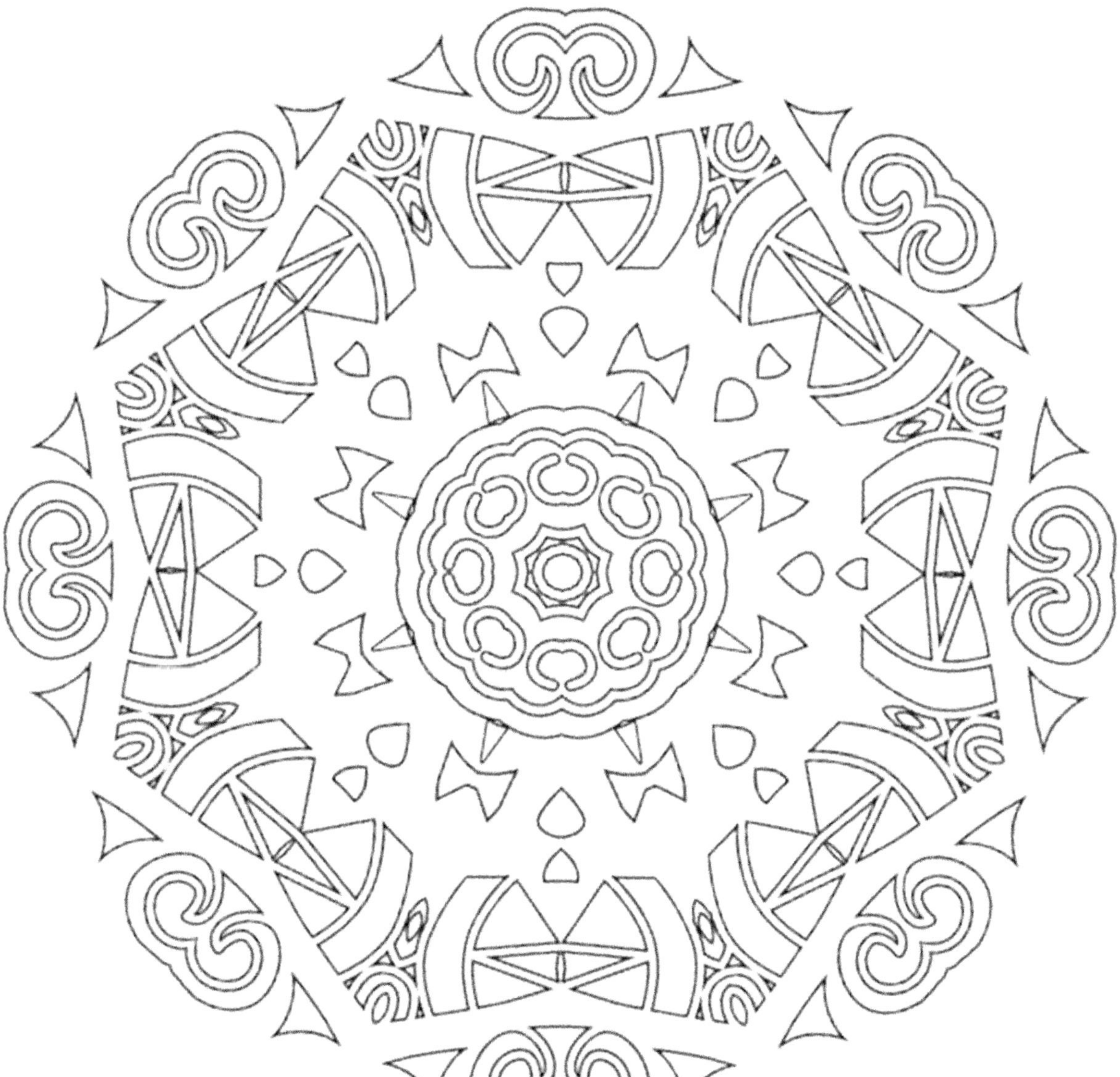

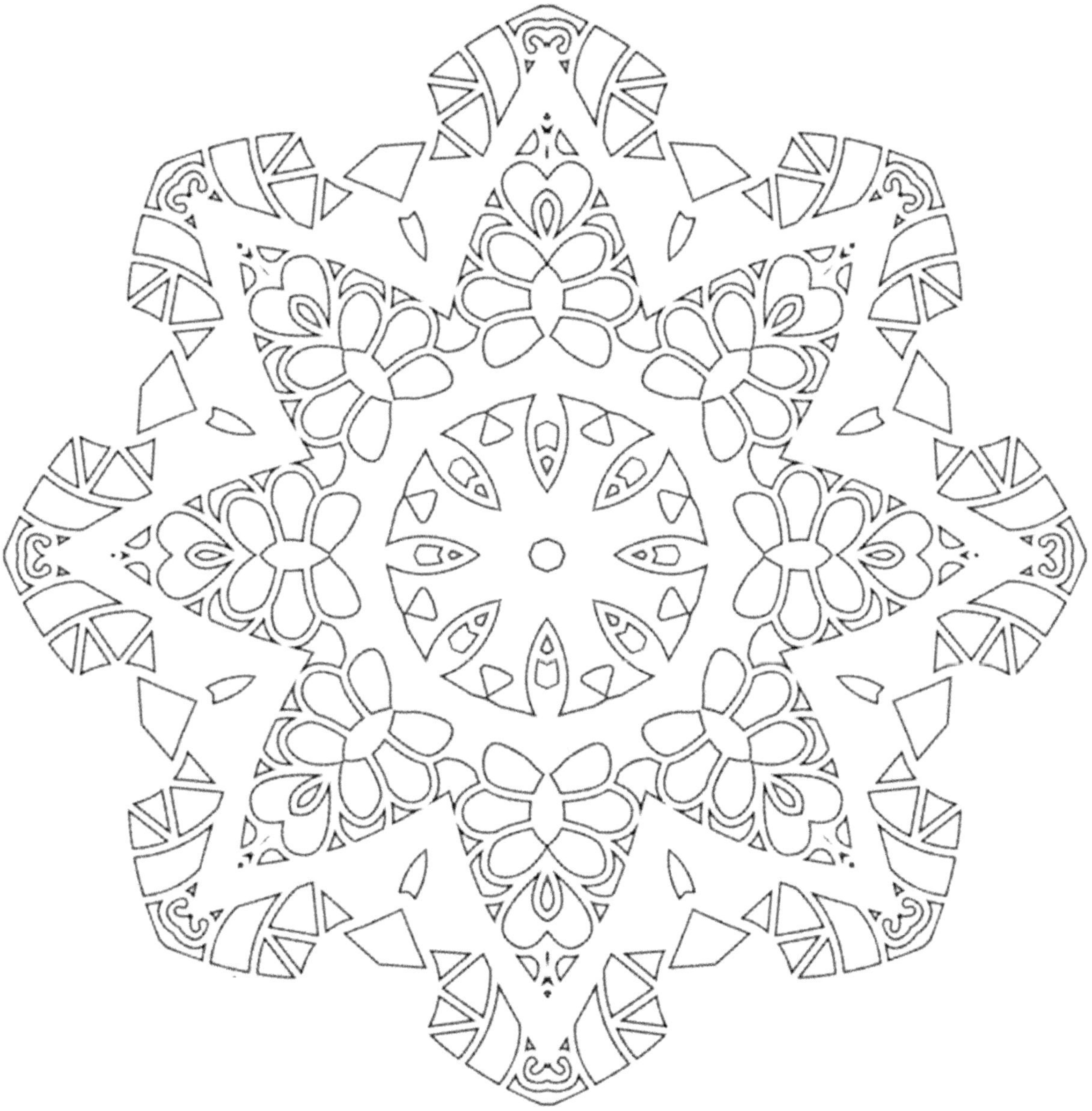

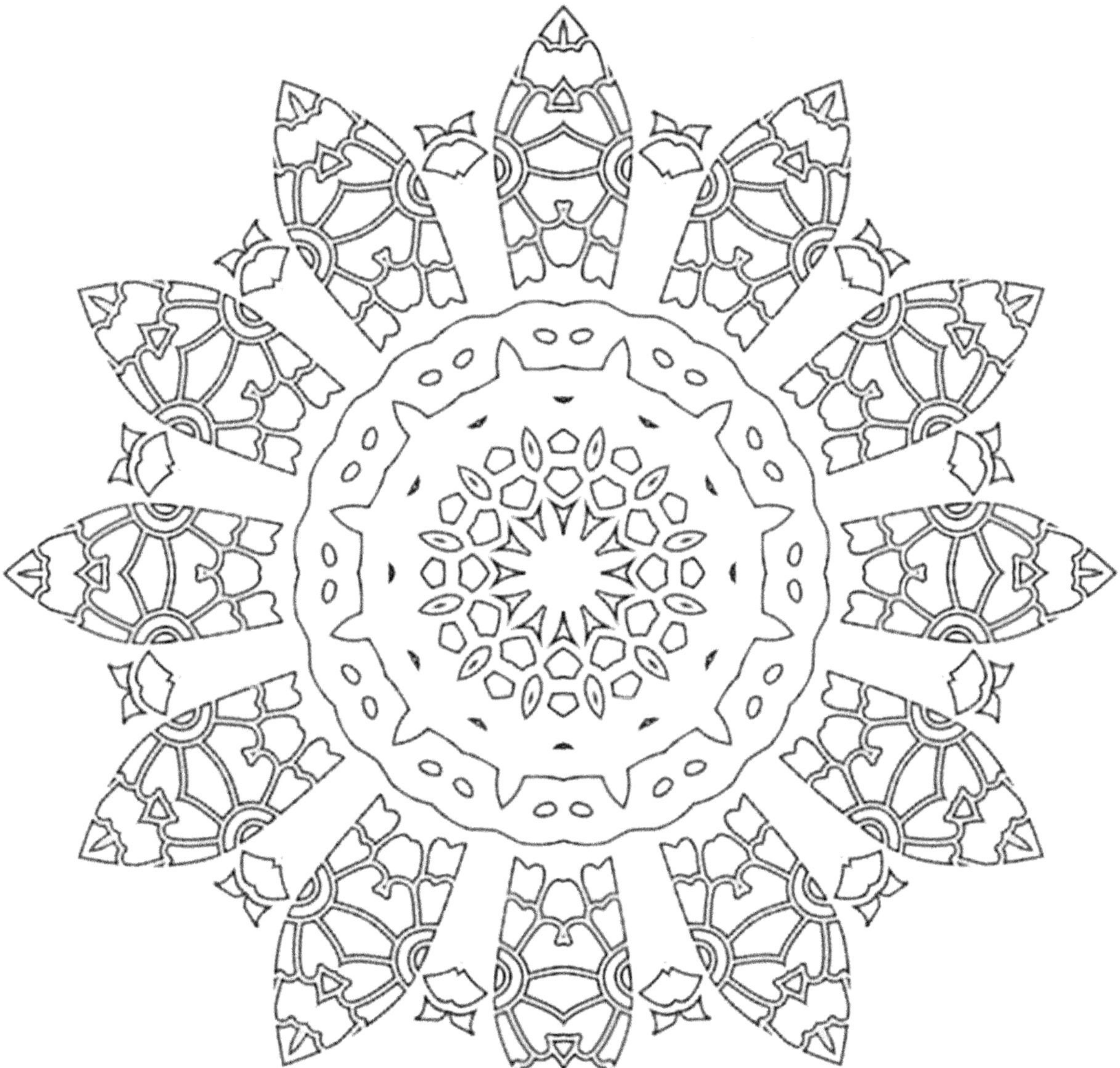

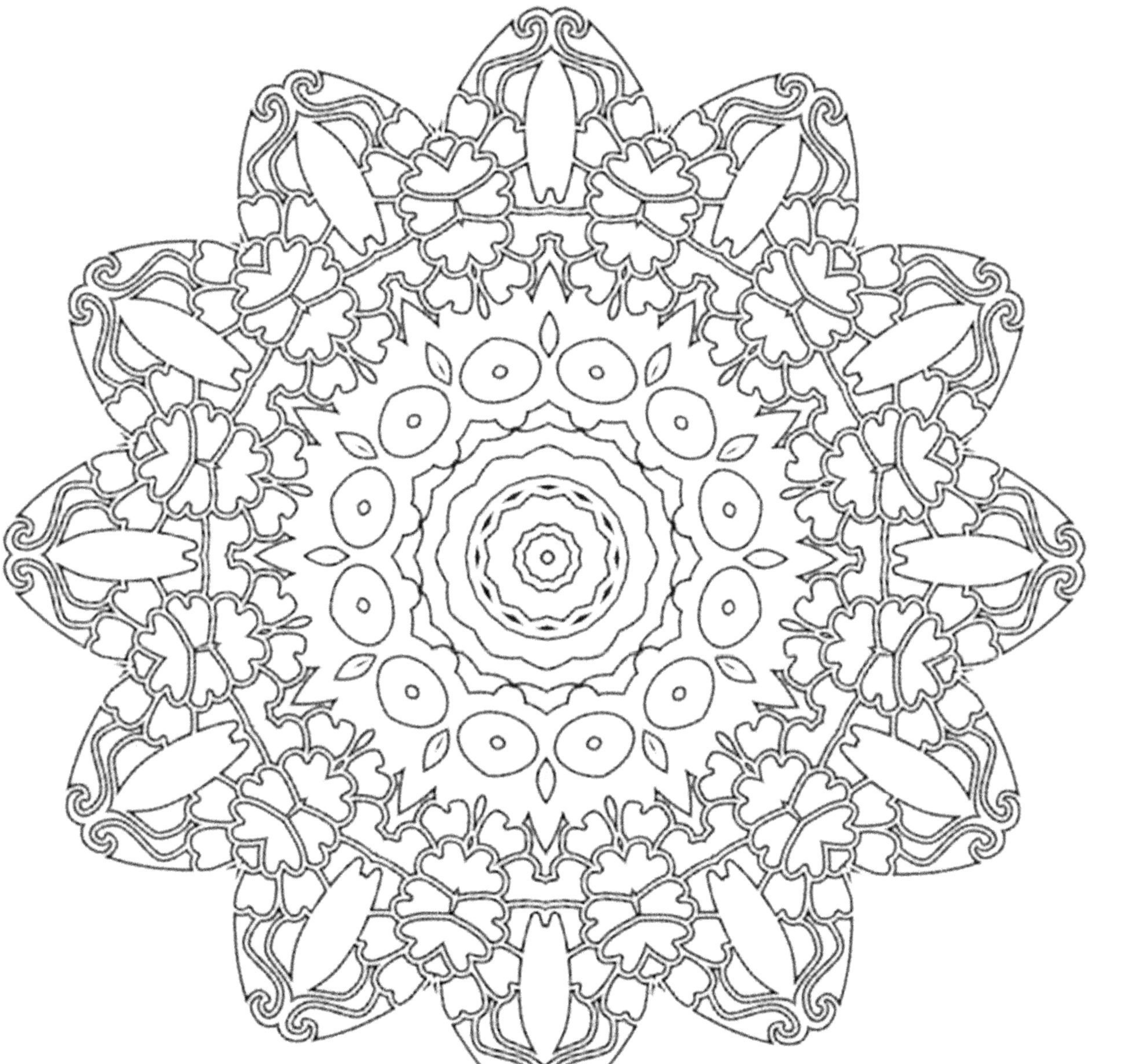

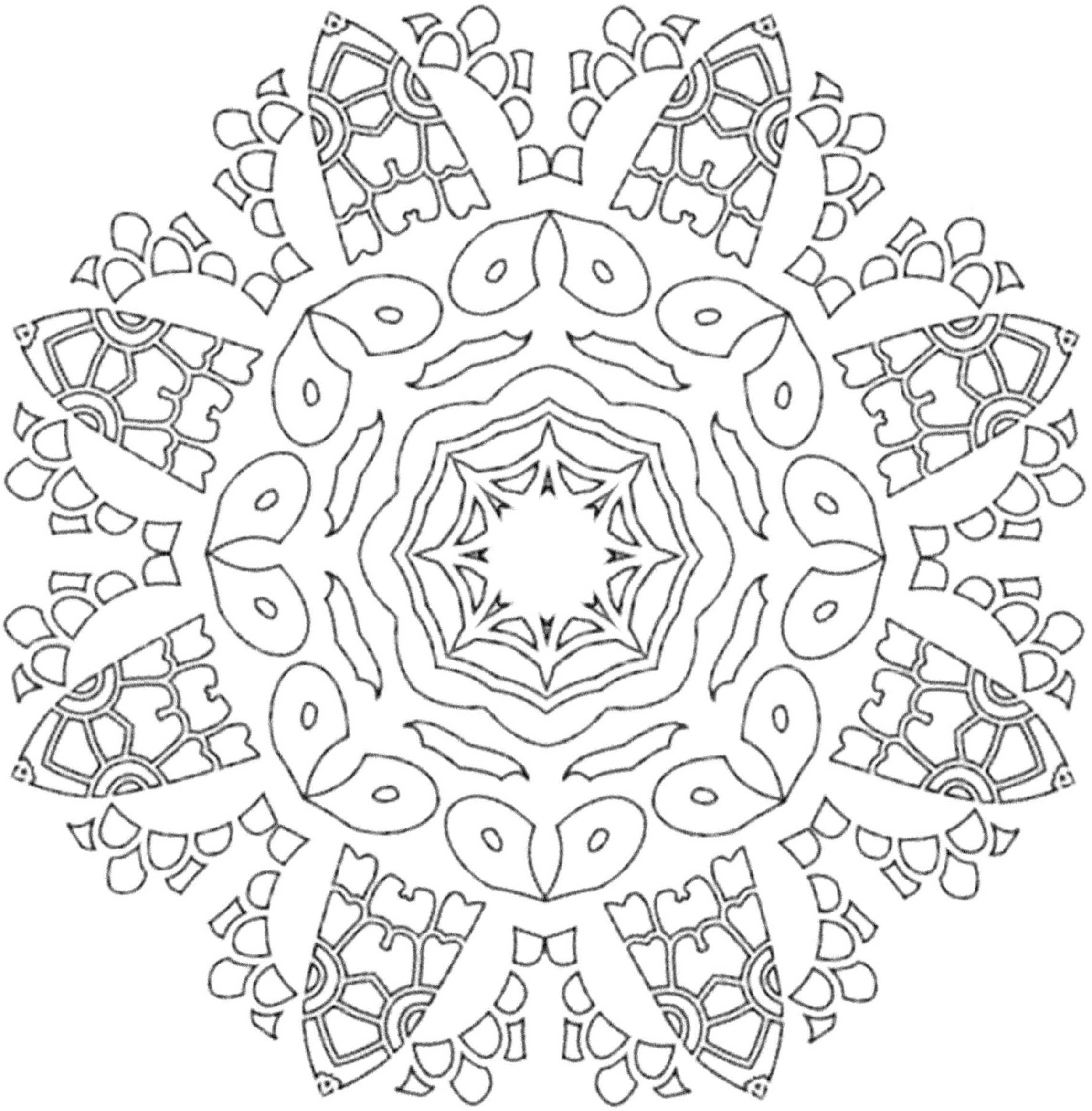

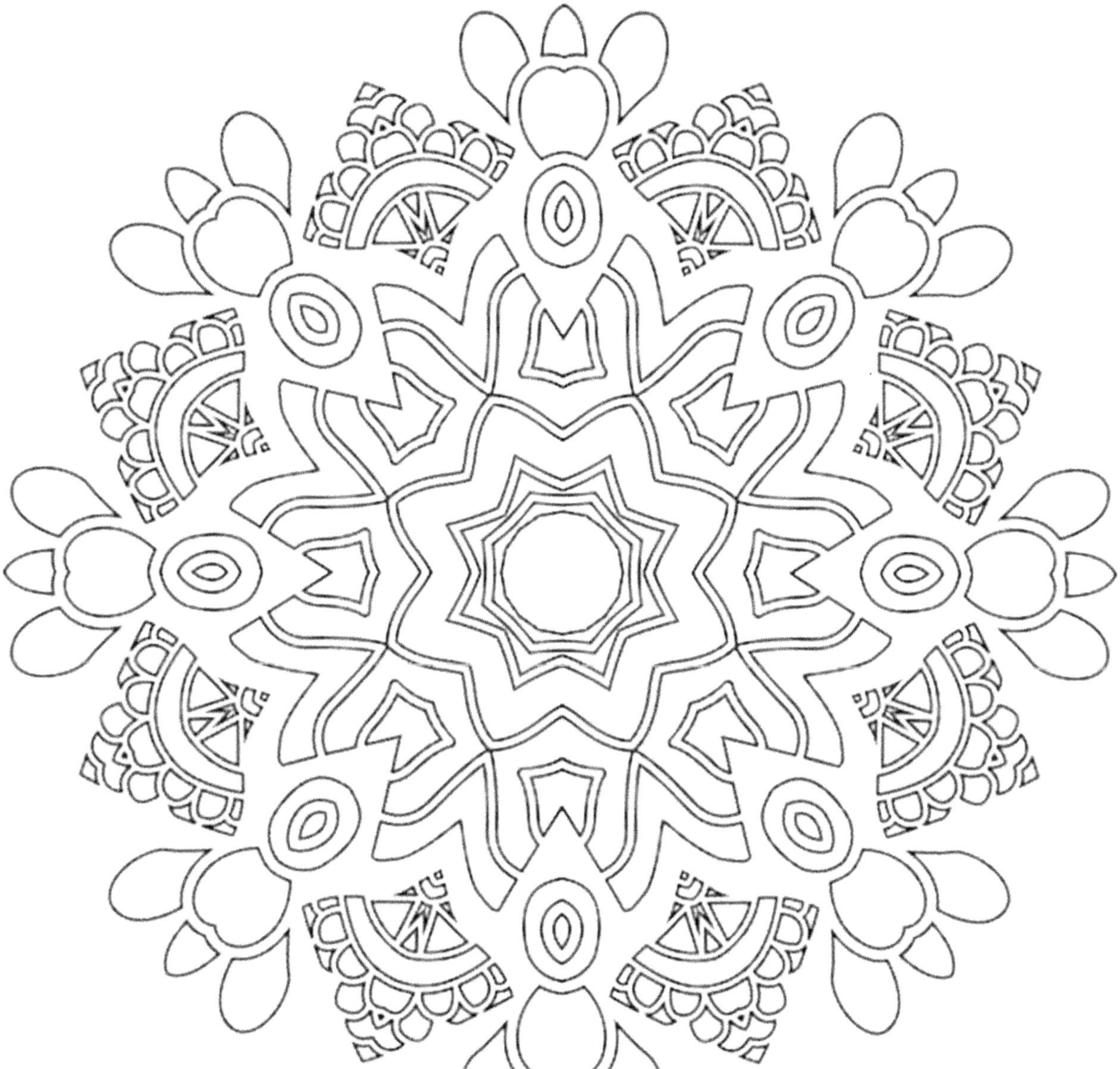

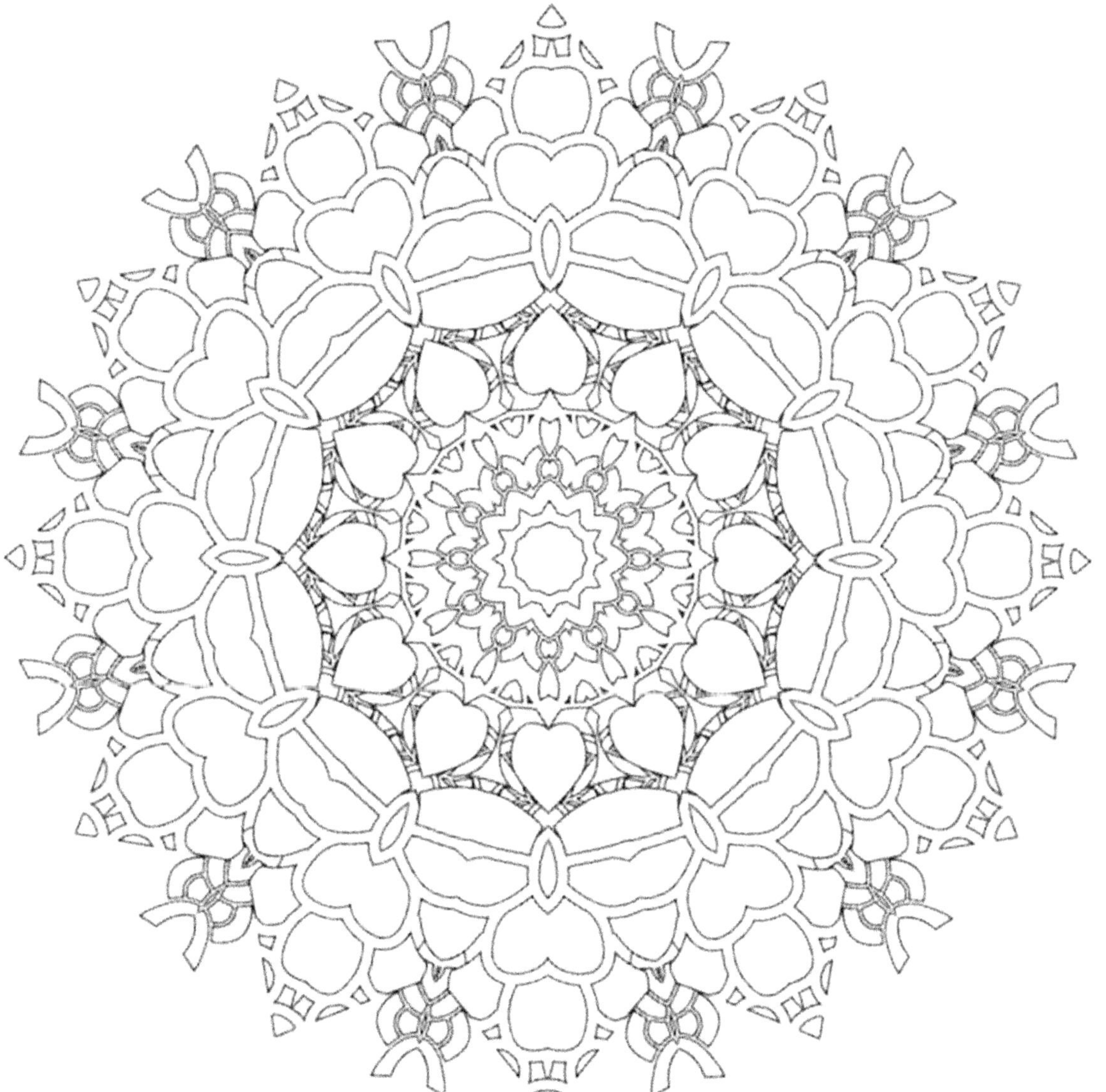

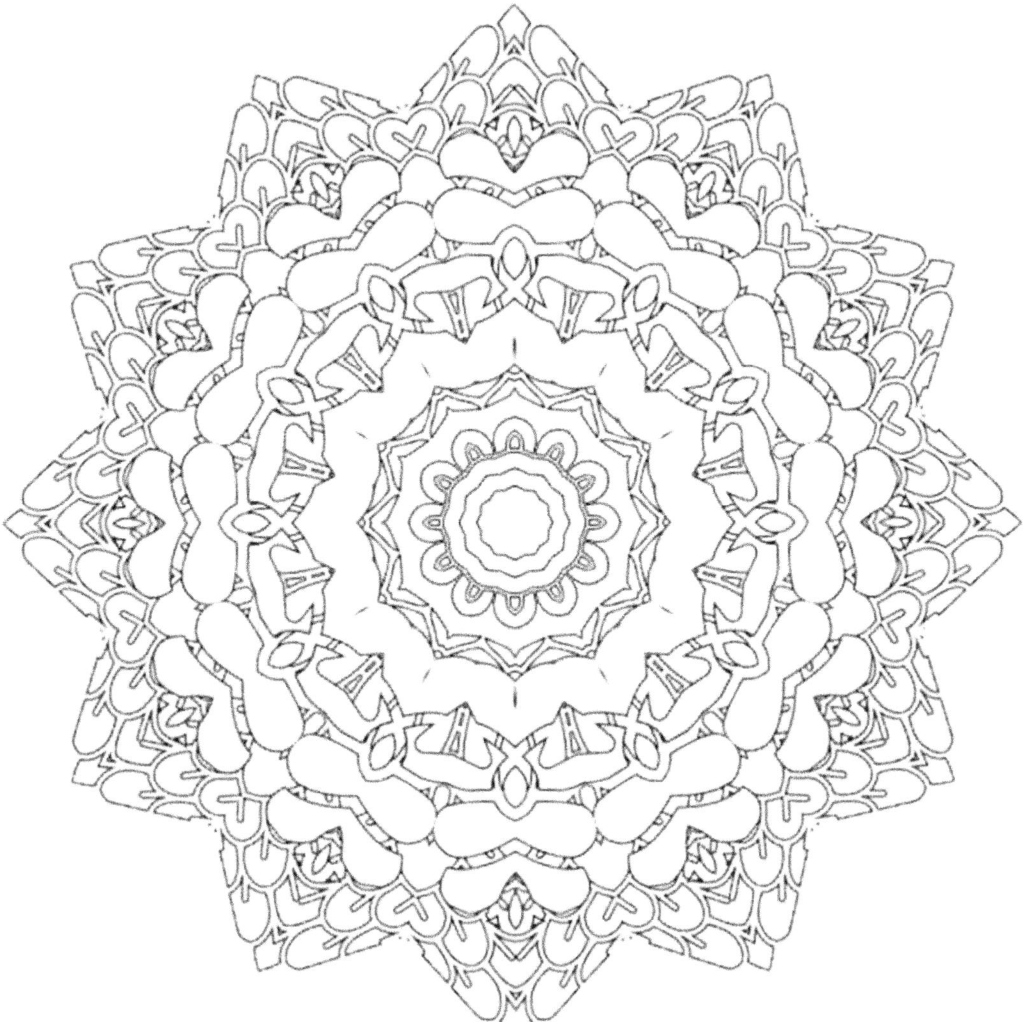

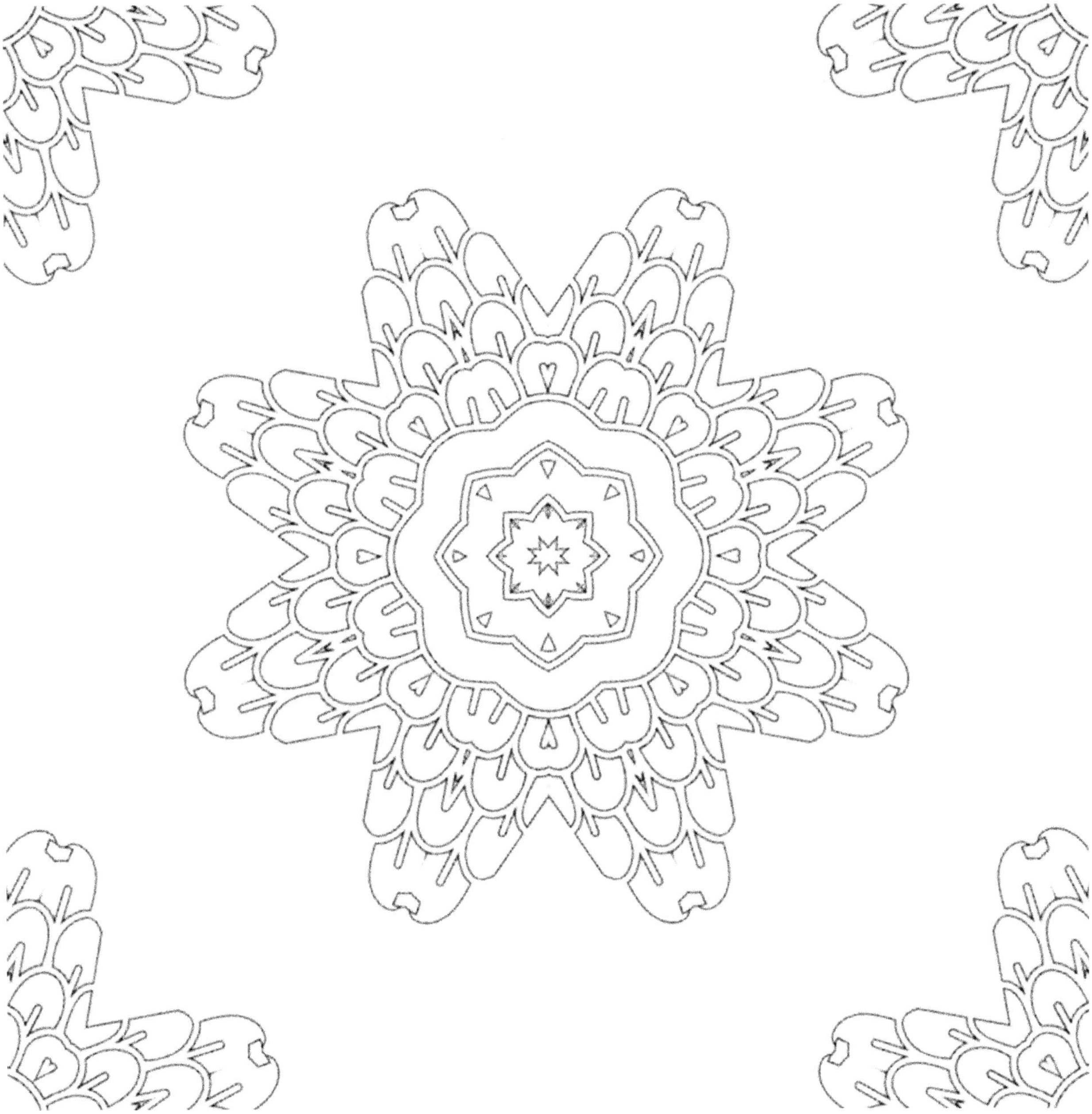

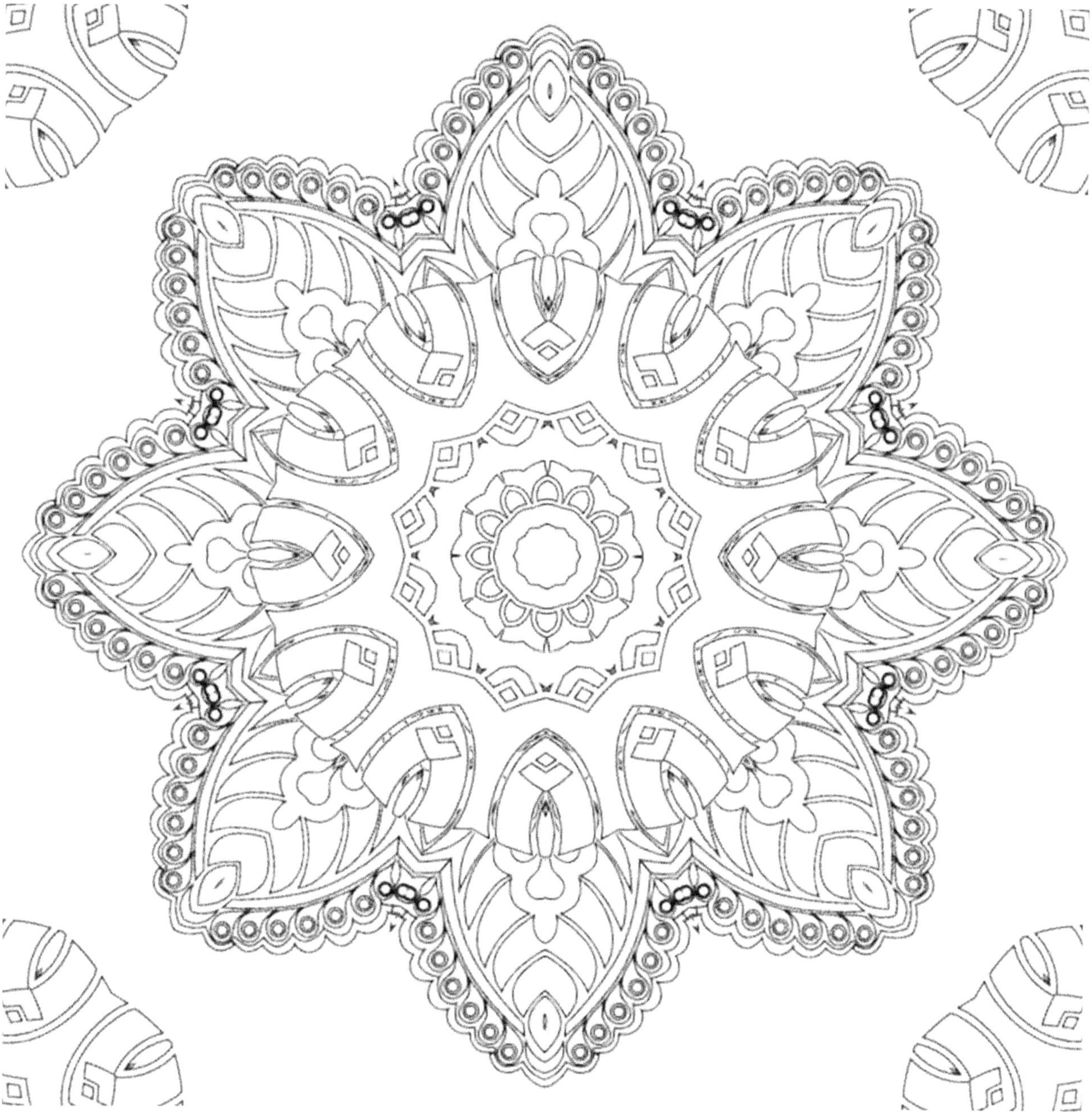

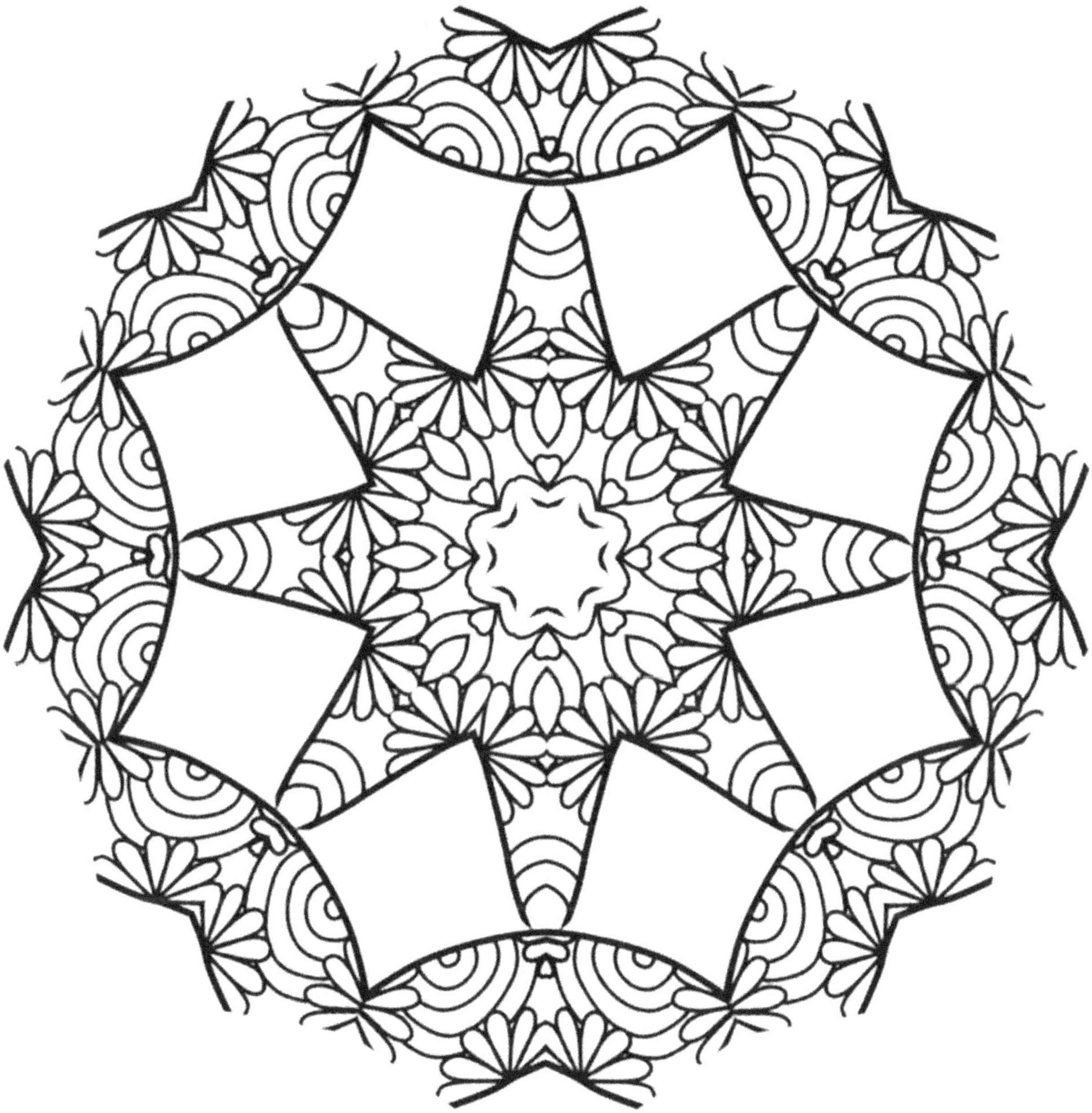

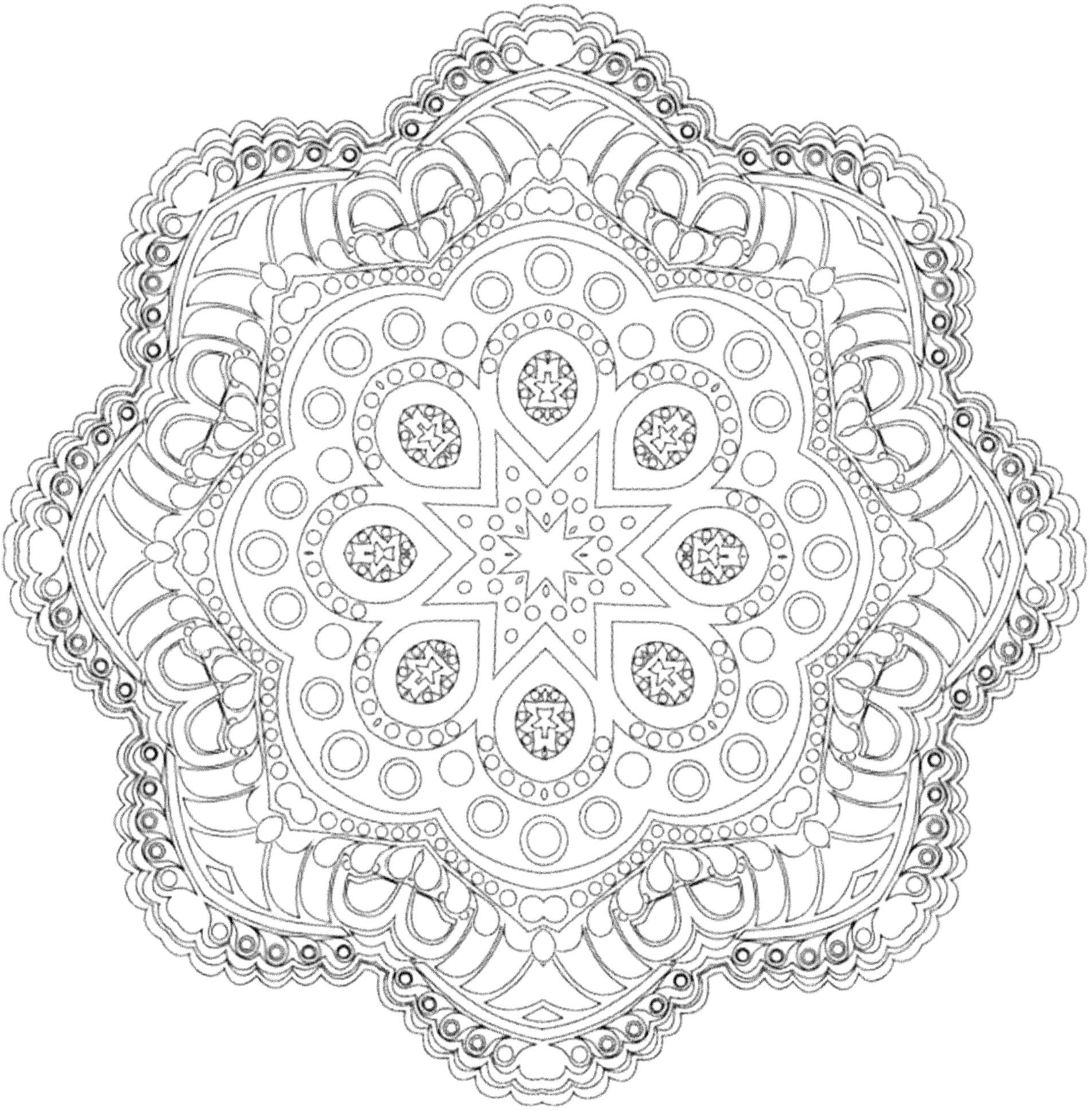

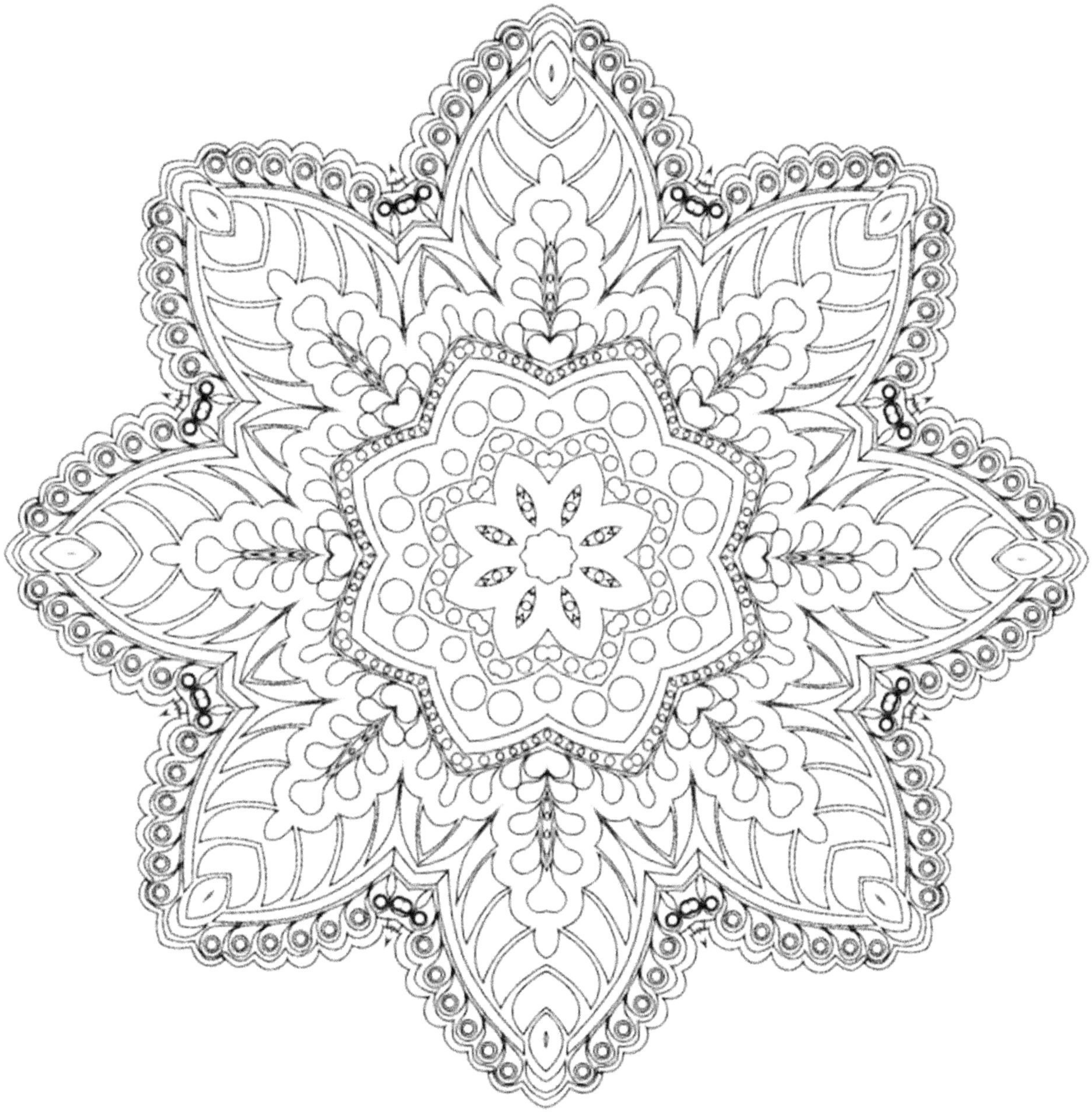

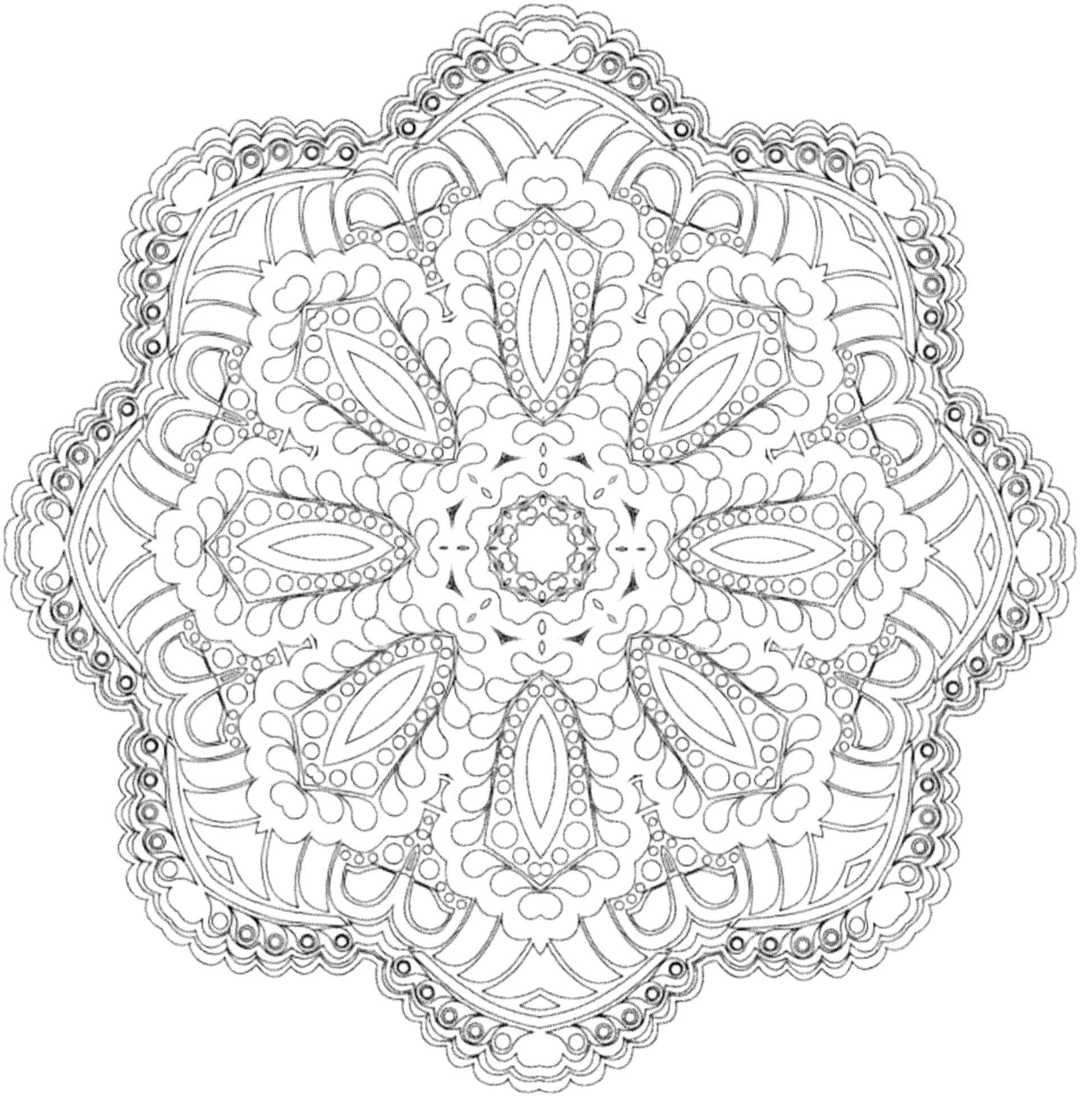

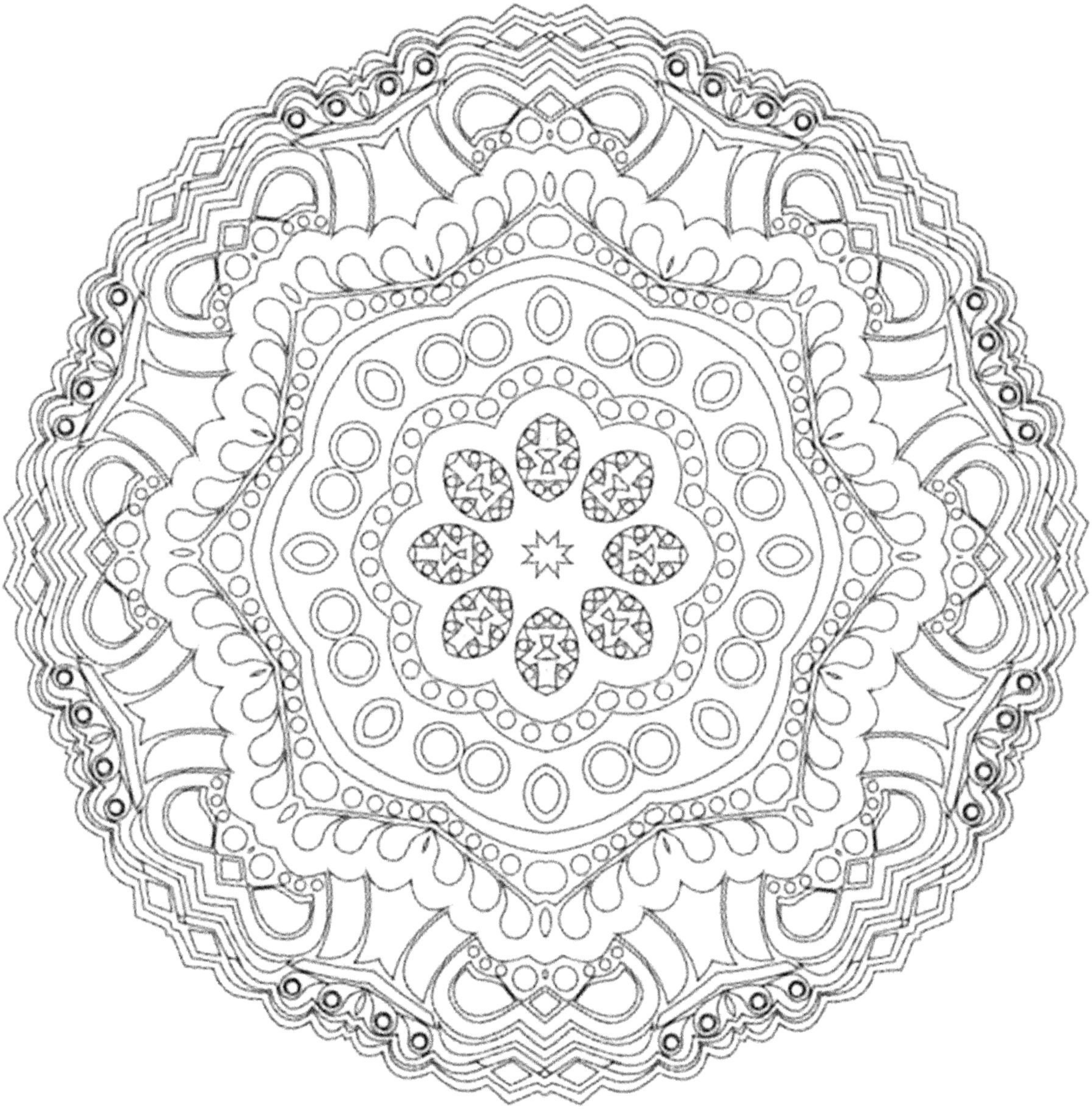

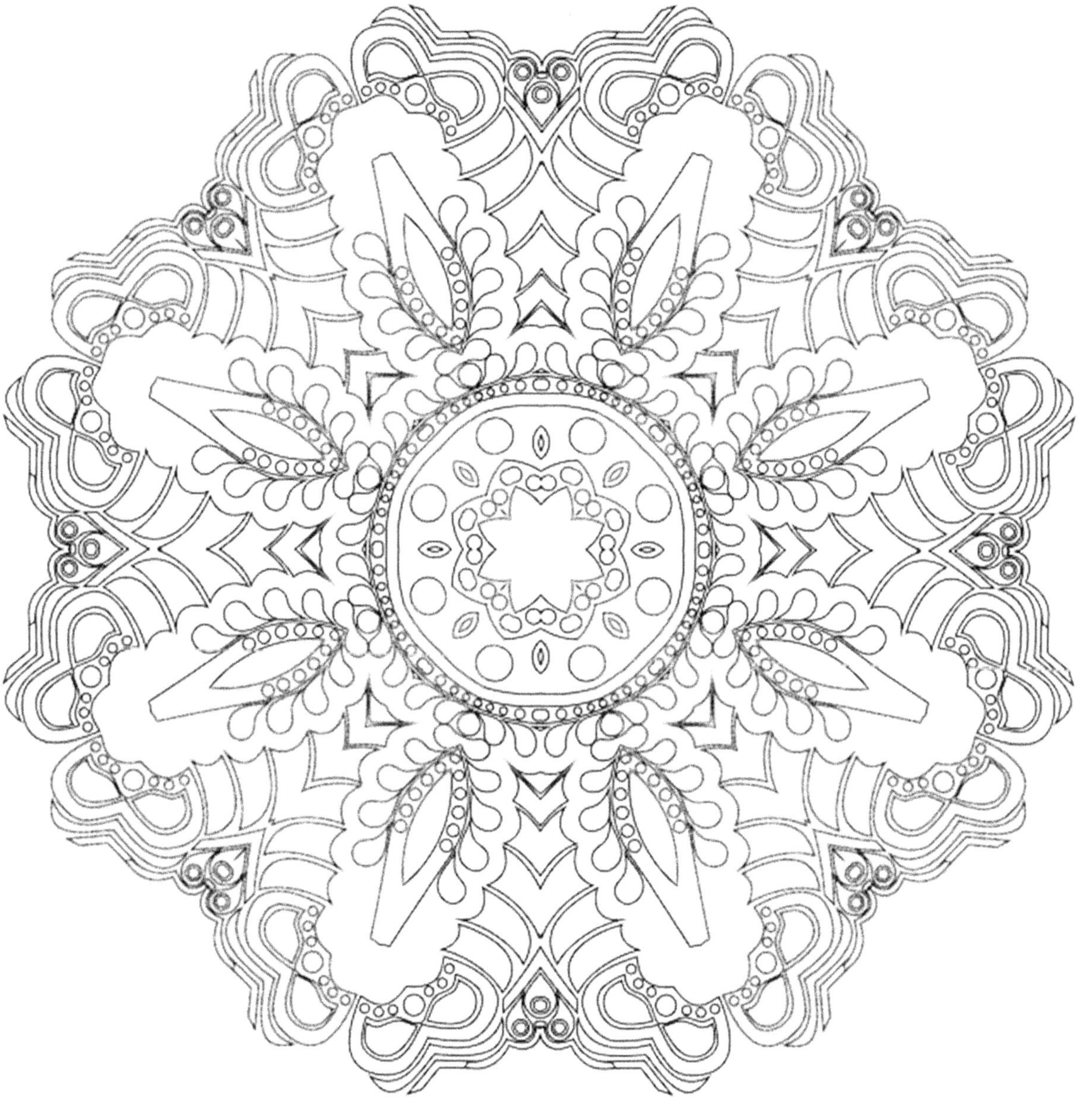

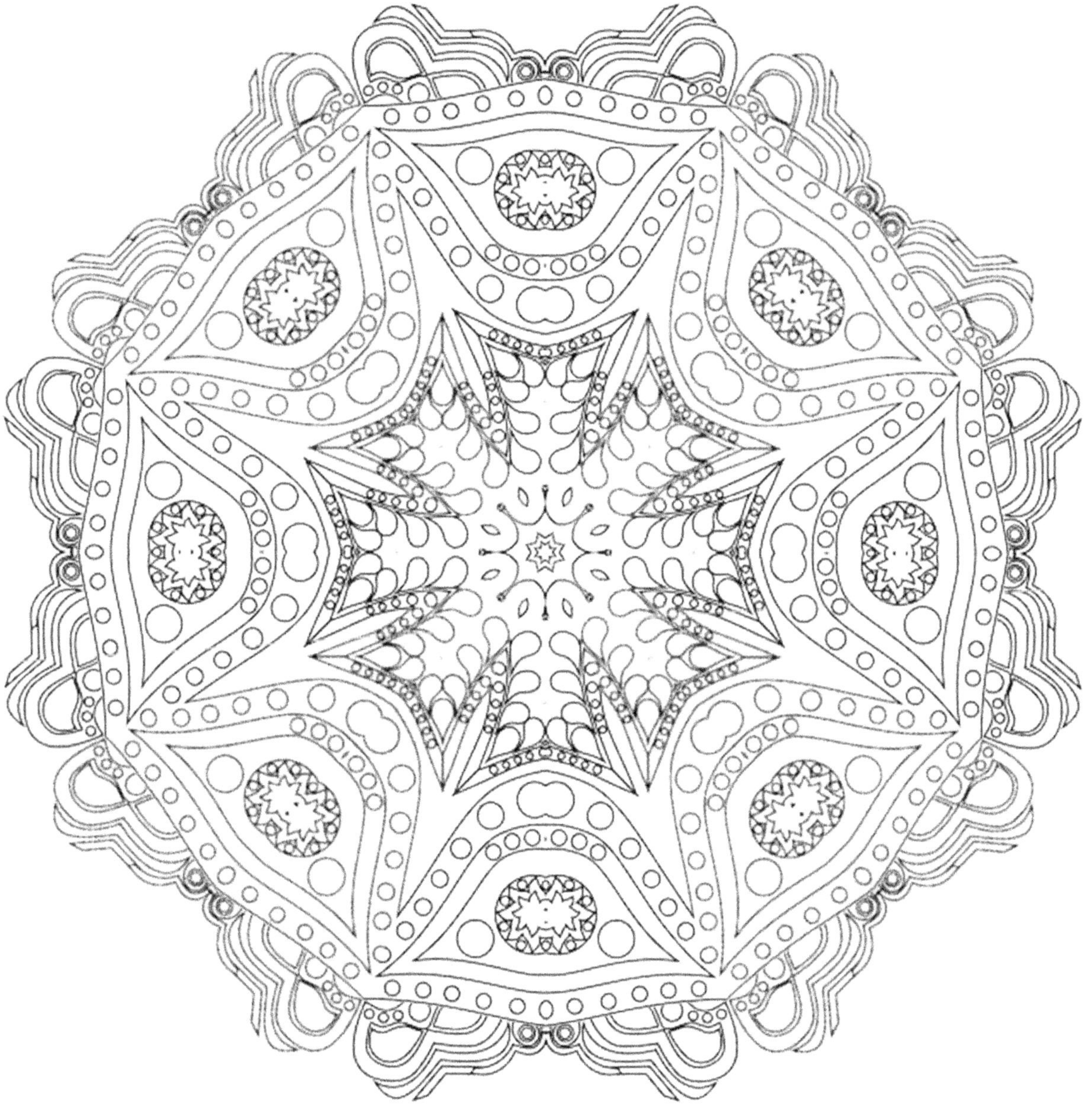

www.ingramcontent.com/pod-product-compliance
Lightning Source LLC
Chambersburg PA
CBHW080553190526
45169CB00007B/2751
9781537350806